Run and not be weary
Spiritual lessons from a would-be runner

© Day One 2022
First printed 2022

ISBN 978-1-84625-734-6

British Library Cataloguing in Publication Data available

Unless otherwise stated, Scripture quotations are from the ESV Bible
(The Holy Bible, English Standard Version), copyright c 2001 by Crossway,
a publishing ministry of Good News Publishers. Used by permission. All
rights reserved.

All opinions and endorsements expressed in this book regarding
running aids are solely the author's and do not necessarily reflect the
views of Day One Publications.

Published by Day One Publications
Ryelands Road, Leominster, HR6 8NZ
email—sales@dayone.co.uk
web site—www.dayone.co.uk

Cover illustration by Kathryn Chedgzoy
Printed by 4edge

Dedication

To my parents, who have both now
completed their spiritual race, but who in
my early years nurtured in me both a love of
running and a love for their Lord and Saviour,
Jesus Christ.

To my husband Michael for his wisdom
and patience, and to my son Nathan and
granddaughter Grace, who inspired me
to realise that it's never too late to start
running.

Endorsements

How do we keep going in the Christian life? It seems to get tougher as the years go by! How helpful then is Karen Worsell's wonderful book urging us to 'run the race marked out for us'. She helpfully draws on her own experiences as one who seeks to run regularly with the challenge of Chronic Fatigue Syndrome, and all firmly anchored in Scripture. Read this and ladle encouragement into your soul.

MIKE MELLOR, PASTOR, EVANGELIST AND AUTHOR, BOURNEMOUTH, ENGLAND

This is a gentle, warm, wise book, blending personal experience with spiritual truth in a way that is sure to help and encourage anyone wanting to run the Christian race with perseverance.

LUKE JENNER, PASTOR, GRACE BAPTIST CHURCH, HALIFAX, ENGLAND

Karen Worsell has written a fabulous little book reflecting on the Christian life as a race. Saturated in Scripture, punctuated by inspiring hymns and populated by godly characters from history, her book follows her project to become a runner at the age of sixty-two. I wholeheartedly recommend it as a devotional resource packed with robust encouragement to run with perseverance the race marked out for us.

DR. RUTH EARDLEY, GP AND MEDICAL JOURNALIST, LEICESTER, ENGLAND

In this encouraging little book, Karen Worsell looks at the many ways in which the Bible compares the Christian life to a race. She illustrates these lessons by drawing on her own experiences both as a runner and a Christian struggling with Chronic Fatigue Syndrome. Being a runner myself, I appreciated the interesting stories from the world of athletics and the practical tips that Karen gives as she describes her own progress from couch to 5K. But the deeper spiritual applications will be a blessing and challenge to anyone seeking to progress on their walk with Christ, regardless of whether they are into running in the physical sense. Karen writes with honesty and realism, encouraging the reader to persevere to the end in their own Christian race.

ELIZABETH EL MOSTAIN, MISSIONARY PASTOR'S WIFE SERVING WITH UFM, MOTHER OF SIX AND AUTHOR OF SURVIVAL TIPS FOR MUMS—PRACTICAL IDEAS FOR THRIVING IN THE EARLY YEARS OF MOTHERHOOD.

A drawing that I did of my first pair of running shoes

Contents

Therefore we also, since we are surrounded by so great a cloud of witnesses, let us lay aside every weight, and the sin which so easily ensnares us, and let us run with endurance the race that is set before us, looking unto Jesus, the author and finisher of our faith, who for the joy that was set before Him endured the cross, despising the shame, and has sat down at the right hand of the throne of God (Hebrews 12:1–2, NKJV).

Train yourself for godliness; for while bodily training is of some value, godliness is of value in every way, as it holds promise for the present life and also for the life to come (1 Timothy 4:7–8).

The authors of the Bible/New Testament use a number of analogies to describe the Christian life. It is likened to a fight; a pilgrimage; a plant growing and producing fruit. It is also described in several passages of Scripture as a *race*. Christian believers are compared to runners in this race, and much is revealed to us in these passages regarding the manner in which we should *run*. One of the most familiar of these verses is Hebrews 12:1: 'Let us run with endurance the race that is set before us.' However, as I have increasingly realized, there are more references to 'running the race' in the Bible than many of us would have first thought. In the coming chapters, I would like to share how the lessons I have been learning as a runner have helped to make such Bible passages more real and meaningful to me.

Many of the thoughts and ideas in this book have come into my mind over the past few weeks and months, as I have been running. Sometimes it was a Bible verse related to running or keeping going in the Christian life; on other occasions it was an insight into one of the principles of running which seemed applicable to our spiritual race as believers in Jesus Christ. These spiritual truths have often inspired me and kept me from giving up part way along one of my more difficult runs, as I have remembered and repeated to myself such verses as 'I press on towards the goal for the prize of the upward call of God in Christ Jesus' (Philippians 3:14). More importantly, the lessons about running, that I have been learning in a practical way, have been a real spur and help to me as I persevere in my spiritual race. I trust that they will be of some help to you also.

My special thanks go to my sister Lesley for her helpful advice and encouragement in writing this book; to my husband Michael

Introduction

for persevering in running alongside me; and to Grace and Lois, my eldest two granddaughters, who inspired me to realize that it is never too early or too late to become a runner.

🙶 My running story

I was born to run. If anyone had reason to be a natural runner, it was me. My parents were both athletes: my father a keen cross-country runner, and my mother an aspiring sprinter who narrowly missed out on selection for the British team in the 1948 Olympic Games. She was able to say that she had competed in at least one race against the famous Dutch athlete, Fanny Blankers Koen (*The Flying Housewife*), winner of four gold medals in those Games.

I inherited my parents' enthusiasm for athletics and most sporting activities, and as a child always tried so hard to be chosen for the school teams, but almost invariably without success. The one event for which I was ever picked to represent our Junior School at the annual inter-school sports day was the skipping race. I started well, only to recall halfway along the track my mother's advice to tell myself, 'I know I can, I know I can ...', which so disturbed my rhythm that I ended up tripping over the rope and finishing last. At secondary school, my story was the same: maximum effort but mediocre results. I had to eventually accept the fact that I would never be a great athlete. I still enjoyed netball and swimming, in both of which I was reasonably proficient. However, athletics for me was relegated to a spectator sport on television, cheering on my heroes such as Sebastian Coe, Steve Cram, Paula Radcliffe and Brendan Foster with great enthusiasm, rejoicing with them in their moments of medals and glory, and sharing with them their pain on losing.

My Running Story

During my first two years at university, there were a few attempts on my part to jog around the small man-made lake in the grounds of our halls of residence with a few friends or, in my penultimate year of study, to run once a week in a small group led by a couple of super-fit students who were in the Territorial Army; the rest of the group felt a great sense of achievement if we actually succeeded in finishing the course. There was always a part of me that felt a secret longing to be able to run; like Eric Liddell, immortalized in the film *Chariots of Fire*, I felt that somehow if only I could run, then I too would 'feel His pleasure' ('God made me for a purpose, but he also made me fast! And when I run, I feel His pleasure.'—Eric Liddell, Olympic 400m gold medallist, Paris 1924, and later missionary in China).[1]

After finishing my studies, commencing work as a doctor, marrying and having two children, trying to retain some degree of fitness was once more a goal. There were several brief attempts to start running again, but these were usually short-lived and not sustained. Looking back, I think that the reason for my failure to persevere and improve was mainly because of lack of preparation, not building up distance sufficiently slowly, and not running often enough. Frustrated by my lack of progress, I would invariably become discouraged and give up. In my late thirties, I joined a ladies' running group which met at a local sports centre; once a week we would run along the streets of Rochdale, and over a period of three to four months we progressed from running to the end of the road and back on the first evening, to eventually completing a circuit of 3 miles (5km). But even this weekly outing was a major effort for me. I rarely went out on any training runs in-between our weekly group runs, and after a while I stopped attending and gave up running once more.

And then, in my early forties, I gradually began to develop various symptoms, of which the major one was overwhelming fatigue. On most days, I would return home from work, as a part-time General Practitioner, in the early afternoon feeling exhausted and then spend a couple of hours in bed before the children came home from school. This persisted to the extent that, about eighteen months later, I gave in my notice at the surgery, feeling unable to perform my medical duties to an acceptable standard. I had by this time undergone various tests to ascertain the cause of my malaise, and when most of these showed no abnormality, I began to suspect that I might have Chronic Fatigue Syndrome (CFS). I was later referred to a specialist in Liverpool who confirmed this diagnosis, and despite various courses of 'treatment' and much financial expenditure in the attempt to find effective therapy in the years since then, it has remained with me and I am still learning to live with the condition to this day. This illness dealt a real blow to any idea of me ever being able to run again. When the CFS was at its worst, I ached all over and struggled to walk, climb stairs or hills, and just felt like staying in bed much of the day. If walking was difficult, running was out of the question. Thankfully, over the past few years I have made a degree of progress. This improvement began approximately two years ago, partly by taking a daily afternoon walk which initially lasted less than five minutes, but very gradually increased so that after a few months I could manage twenty to thirty minutes walking at a reasonable pace.

Assuming that this level of activity was the best that I could hope for at my age, my aim was simply to maintain this degree of fitness into my sixties and hopefully beyond. However, a further twist in my story came while on a New Year break with my husband, Michael, a little over twelve months ago. Drinking a welcome coffee after a morning of exploring the shops in Harrogate, we received a phone message with an attached photograph of our son and his ten-year-old daughter, with the caption, 'Just completed our first 5K Parkrun!' Initially thinking this was some kind of joke, we later realized that they were serious, and had actually entered the run at a local park without telling us beforehand. I said nothing more on the subject to my husband at the time, but in my mind there rose a faint glimmer of hope, that perhaps, just possibly, there might be a slight chance that even *I* could join my son and granddaughter on one of these Parkruns one day.

The photo that started it all. Grace with my son, Nathan.

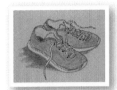 My spiritual journey

As well as both being runners, my parents were also committed Christians. From my earliest days I was taken to church and heard the message of the Bible. I knew that there was a God who created the world, that mankind had sinned and gone astray from God, and that God had sent His Son, Jesus Christ, to die on the cross, to bear the punishment for my wrongdoing. I can remember on a number of occasions asking God to forgive me, but afterwards never having any real assurance that He had done so.

As I reached my teens, with the consequent self-awareness and questioning, I struggled with the idea that perhaps I only believed these 'truths' because I had been repeatedly taught them. Was Christianity really true, and if so, was *I* a real Christian? I had certainly asked God for forgiveness many times, but had He heard me? Had my prayers made any difference to my life? I heard testimonies of people whose lives had been suddenly and dramatically changed by trusting in Jesus, and somehow expected this to happen to me. Disappointed by the lack of this sort of *Damascus Road* experience, I doubted at times whether I was genuinely converted or *born again*. I did not turn away from God or reject the Bible's teaching; I believed it and continued to try to follow Christ. I was baptized in my local church at the age of sixteen and sought to share my faith with friends and acquaintances, even going on two weeks of beach mission in the summer before starting university.

The turning point in my assurance of salvation was a gradual one, brought about mainly by a clearer understanding of Biblical truth. It certainly began while still living at home but was helped greatly at university by regular attendance at a church that clearly taught the Bible's message. I came to see that it was entirely by faith in God's promises, based on Jesus Christ's completed work on the cross, that I was saved. It was not by looking constantly to my feelings, or checking my 'spiritual pulse' excessively, but simply looking to Christ and knowing that He had done everything that was necessary for my forgiveness. 1 John 1:9 states that, 'If we confess our sins, he (God) is faithful and just to forgive us our sins, and to cleanse us from *all* unrighteousness.' I realized that if God had promised it, I needed to believe it! I knew that I *was* one of Christ's sheep, of whom He had said, 'My sheep hear my voice, and I know them, and they follow me. I give them eternal life, and they will never perish, and no one will snatch them out of my hand' (John 10:27–28). Along with the realization of these truths came a new peace and security, a joy that stemmed from the knowledge that nothing '... in all creation will be able to separate us from the love of God in Christ Jesus our Lord' (Romans 8:39).

It would be great if I could say that from then until now, over forty years later, my Christian pathway has been easy and smooth, always walking closely with the Lord in obedience to His commands. But that would, by no means, be true. What I can say is that God is faithful, and has graciously kept me through many trials, and much stumbling on my part, until this day.

Whatever happens in this life, we are told that nothing can '... separate us from the love of God in Christ Jesus our Lord' (Romans 8:38–39).

'And I am sure of this, that He who began a good work in you will bring it to completion at the day of Jesus Christ' (Philippians 1:6).

1 Preparation

At the age of sixty-two and with a twenty-year history of CFS, any attempt on my part to begin as a runner, and in particular any hope of succeeding to continue in this activity, would depend largely on two things: my motivation, and my preparation.

Motivation was not a major problem for me; since childhood I had always possessed an innate desire to run. True, there were periods in my past when this longing had been suppressed or felt to be unattainable, but it had never been fully extinguished. When I heard of my ten-year-old granddaughter's running participation, that desire was quickly rekindled, and I determined to take things further.

What I needed, therefore, was to prepare. Prior to this point I had been going for a brisk half-hour walk most afternoons for some months, but to progress from this level of activity to starting to actually run seemed to me like a quantum leap. In my mind and with my medical knowledge, suffering from CFS equated to being unable to achieve any such degree of physical output. I had been repeatedly informed that if I used up too much of my limited pot of energy, I was likely to suffer for it for several days or weeks afterwards, with a flare-up of my Chronic Fatigue symptoms. I had been advised about 'pacing', or as the Americans called it, 'living within your energy envelope', and certainly did not wish to exacerbate my CFS by any sudden increase in activity. I knew, therefore, that I must find out all I could about how to start and very gradually progress in running in a sustainable way, so that I did not give up after a few weeks, as on previous occasions. Ideally, I needed to find a running course or programme that would take me step by step (literally) from being a total beginner, to eventually becoming a regular, consistent runner. This is where such programmes as *Couch to 5K* (C25K) and *None to Run* (*N2R*) sounded so helpful; I could simply read the advice they gave, then put on my headphones as I commenced a run (or run/walk initially) and carry out the instructions to 'Start walking', 'Start running slowly', or (best of all), 'You've completed your run. Good job!' Having looked at the *Couch to 5k* programme with its claims of enabling absolute beginners (couch potatoes) to be able to run for 5k or thirty minutes at the end of nine weeks, by running three times a week in gradually increasing increments, and having discussed it with my husband Michael, we decided to start on the course together.

Before even setting off on a running programme, I researched what running shoes would be best for me, the right type of clothing to wear, what food I should eat (and when), how often to run, and anything that I needed to stop doing or adjust in my daily routine, to succeed as a runner. This was serious; I desperately wanted to achieve my goal and was willing to do whatever it took to obtain it. Having looked up online the 'Ten best running shoes for women' (how did we manage before the internet?), I ordered a pair from the list that were not (too) expensive. A short-sleeved running top or vest for the warmer weather, plus a long-sleeved top and a lightweight waterproof for colder or rainy days were purchased, along with long jogging trousers and shorts. A special belt with zip pockets to carry my phone and keys looked a good idea and was also bought.

I also considered my diet and eating habits. I was not, strictly speaking, overweight, but over the previous few years had slowly gained about a stone in weight (5–6Kg). This had not been helped by my suffering from CFS for so long, which meant that much of the time I had not had sufficient energy to be as physically active as I would have wished. I had maintained the same calorie intake, however, which had allowed the weight to creep on, particularly since the menopause. I sought to address this by looking at my daily diet and deciding to cut out the crisps, biscuits, cakes and high calorie puddings which were my weakness; stick to low calorie desserts; and increase the quantity of healthier items such as fruit, vegetables and protein that I consumed. The only *treat* I continued to permit myself was a small daily ration of eighty-five per cent dark chocolate, which I was sure had plenty of health benefits!

Other questions that arose included: Was I regularly obtaining sufficient good quality sleep? How frequently should I run? When was the best time of day to run? This led me into consideration of my daily routine, particularly once I had commenced the running programme. I realized that I needed to try and maintain regular hours for rising and for going to bed each day, allowing sufficient time between eating a meal and setting off on a run, and taking time to perform warm-up exercises immediately before running, to reduce the risk of sprains and injury.

Why mention all these details? Because setting out on the race as a Christian is a much more serious, life-changing matter. If careful thought is necessary before deciding to take up running, how much more so is this true for the spiritual realm. Running the Christian race affects our whole life, or should I say, it *is* our life. It requires discipline and self-sacrifice. Jesus himself warned his followers:

Whoever does not bear his own cross and come after me cannot be my disciple. For which of you, desiring to build a tower, does not first sit down and count the cost, whether he has enough to complete it? (Luke 14:27–28).

We are told to put aside sin and everything that hinders:

Let us also lay aside every weight, and sin which clings so closely, and let us run with endurance the race that is set before us (Hebrews 12:1).

The apostle Paul reminded the believers in Lystra, Iconium and Antioch that: '... through many tribulations we must enter the kingdom of God' (Acts 14:22).

Sadly, the cost of discipleship is not always clearly spelt out by many preachers. Such men tell their hearers that all they have to do is 'come to Christ', all their problems will disappear, and they will live happily ever after. Then, when those who respond to such a message encounter difficulties in the race, they become discouraged and may even give up altogether. If only they had been given the whole picture, that the Christian life is not an easy race and that it can be at times a great struggle. We have an enemy, the devil, who tries all means to make us stumble and fall, so that we do not reach the finishing line. But we also have a Saviour, the Lord Jesus Christ, who is able to keep us from stumbling; and we will surely know that the race has all been worth it on that great day when we are presented '... blameless before the presence of his glory with great joy' (Jude v. 24).

Thinking specifically about our daily routine and its importance in being able to run successfully, this also has a parallel in preparing for our spiritual race. If we overslept, jumped out of bed late and hurriedly gobbled down our breakfast, rushed out of the front door in our pyjamas and slippers and expected to be able to run effortlessly along our intended route, we would be disappointed. It would not work (and we might also get a few odd looks from passers-by). In a similar way, we should not expect to be able to run well in spiritual terms and live in a way that is pleasing to God if we do not get up at a reasonable hour and spend time with God at the beginning of each day. Reading and meditating on some verses from the Bible to see what God has to say to us, and talking to God in prayer, are vital, to be prepared for whatever part of the race we have before us for the rest of that day. The Christian life is compared elsewhere in Scripture to a battle, with the devil being our enemy. We are told, in Ephesians 6:11, to 'put on the whole armour of God', so that we will be able to withstand the devil's attacks. We can do nothing in our own strength, only with the help of the Holy Spirit. Only by seeking God's presence and help for the task can we hope to know spiritual victories and remain on our feet. And yet, how often we seem to be in such a rush to be getting on with life's daily duties, without much more than a quick glance at a few Bible verses and perhaps a short, hurried prayer beforehand. It is little surprise, then, that we often fail to make much spiritual progress. God has given us all that we need to live for Him and run well; let us take every opportunity to use the means He has given us to draw close to Him.

> I do not run aimlessly; I do not box as one beating the air. But I discipline my body and keep it under control, lest after preaching to others I myself should be disqualified (1 Corinthians 9:26–27).

Preparation beforehand is therefore vital, but there comes a moment when we take our first steps and the race really begins. For Michael and I, that moment happened to be on a cold, late January morning in 2020, when we started on day one of the *Couch to 5k* programme. After a five-minute warm-up walk, we ran (slowly) for one minute followed by ninety seconds walking and repeated this pattern for twenty minutes. Initially, even this small amount of running required significant effort for me, but I completed the first week's schedule and it felt good to have made a start.

Thinking of the Christian life as a race, therefore, it also must have a starting point. Is every human being automatically in the race? If not, how does someone enter for and begin this race? In athletics, to enter an event in the Olympic Games or World Championships, an athlete needs to have reached a qualifying standard and entered trials to prove their ability, before being chosen to represent their country. But in total contrast to this, to enter the Christian race requires only that a person turns from their past wrongdoing and puts their trust completely in Jesus Christ for forgiveness of their sins. God does not accept someone because of their good deeds or charitable giving, but simply because His Son, Jesus, took the punishment for their sin when He died on the cross. By admitting our guilt to God and asking Him for mercy, we can be sure that He will hear us. 'If we confess our sins, He is faithful and just to forgive us our sins and to cleanse us from *all* unrighteousness' (1 John 1:9). Having been forgiven and made new, we are ready to start running the Christian race. We now desire to please God by obeying His commands and living holy lives, out of thankfulness for what He has done for us. He gives us His Holy Spirit to enable us to live lives that are pleasing to God, to run the race set before us.

Chapter 1

Run the straight race through God's good grace,

Lift up thine eyes and seek His face;

Life with its path before thee lies,

Christ is the way, and Christ the prize.

(John Samuel Bewley Monsell, 1811–75; from the hymn 'Fight the good fight').

2 The prize

What makes people want to take up running—what is the point?

For many runners, there are likely to be several reasons why they took up this form of physical activity. At the top level of athletics, there may certainly be an element of pride in success and achievements, and the desire to be 'number one' in their chosen field. Many of these talented athletes are now professionals, having gained financial sponsorship, and spend most of their time in training, their goal being to win major races in events such as the Olympics, World Championships and Diamond league events. They run, not just to represent their country, but for personal gain and glory; to win gold medals; to be the best. Some successful athletes appear to love being famous and idolized by their fans, and also seem to enjoy the huge wealth that nowadays accompanies such celebrity status.

For the vast majority of us, however, without the innate speed of the top athletes, running is more likely to be chosen to attain a degree of fitness, to aid in losing excess weight, to improve our mental health, or simply to experience the joy of being a runner. Even so, to succeed at whatever level, there is a need for every runner to have a specific goal or target to aim for. Our goal might be to complete a marathon or 10k race in six months' time or, perhaps more realistically for some, to finish a local 5k run. We aim to be the best that we can be, with the physical health and strength that we have been given.

Chapter 2

When I began running almost ~~one year~~ 3 years ago, I set myself an initial target of running continuously for twenty minutes by the date of my sixty-third birthday, roughly five months later. I set out on the *Couch to 5K* programme in late January; after a week and a half of the programme, I managed to sprain a ligament in my right knee, requiring physiotherapy and four weeks break from running—not the best of starts. Undeterred however, I started again from the beginning of the programme in early March, by which time Michael was on about week six and disappearing into the distance as I struggled to keep running for ninety seconds at a time. I progressed slowly, often taking two or three weeks for one particular week of the course because of how difficult I was finding it. To run for three minutes at a time before walking again was hard work, and day one of the following week (week five of the programme) I was supposed to run for five minutes at a time, repeated three more times, with a short walk between each run; by the end of week five I was apparently going to run for twenty minutes without stopping! After three weeks stuck on Week Four and feeling unable to progress further, I began to get disheartened. I searched online once more for further assistance and found that there were a significant number of other people who, like me, had struggled with the *Couch to 5K* course, finding it progressed too quickly for them. I discovered *None2Run* (*N2R*), a programme started by a Canadian runner and coach called Mark Kennedy. This had similar aims to *Couch to 5K*, but differed in content, taking twelve weeks instead of nine to progress to running 5K, and including regular strength and mobility exercises in the training in order to reduce the risk of injury. Added to this was the opportunity to correspond by email with the programme founder and obtain help and advice during the programme if needed.

Having checked the details of what was expected week by week on the *N2R* programme, I decided that starting on week five was a realistic aim, and so I set out ... again. This time, despite having to repeat the odd week to be on the safe side, I found that I was able to keep up more easily with the weekly increments; there was still one jump (from week nine to ten) which entailed increasing from five-minute running intervals to twenty minutes running without a break, but I was assured that the difficulty in making this jump was more a mental block than a physical one. On the day of my birthday, I set off steadily and to my surprise managed to run for the full twenty minutes, even though halfway through the run the heavens opened and there was a torrential downpour, which lasted until the end of the course. I returned home completely drenched but wildly elated at my achievement—one which six months earlier had seemed an impossible dream.

Having succeeded in overcoming this hurdle, I gained a new confidence that I could now run gradually longer distances and persevere as a runner. Since then, I have successfully completed the *N2R* programme and now regularly run 4–5K, two or three times per week. I continue to set new goals to aim for, my current one being to run 5K in thirty minutes. My original aim to be able to complete a 5K Parkrun with my son and granddaughter is still to be fulfilled, because all Parkruns in the UK were cancelled last Spring due to Covid-19 and are still not happening at the time of writing, but I hope that I will have the opportunity to achieve this in a few months' time, when lockdown restrictions are eased(*see postscript).

Chapter 2

There are still days when running is a real effort, but more often than not I do actually enjoy it! There is something special about running along the canal in the picturesque countryside near home on a still, sunny autumn morning when it feels good to be alive. Quite frequently I will spot a heron perched on the edge of the canal or, on rare occasions, catch a glimpse of a kingfisher swiftly skimming the surface of the water. But even if I am not so fortunate or the weather is miserable, I am still glad that I can now call myself a runner.

While there may be various answers given to the question of why a person runs, the most obvious reason, then, is that we want to achieve our goal. Spiritually, our aim or goal as a Christian is to finish the race, and to receive the prize. In a physical race, the only person who wins the race is the one who crosses the finishing line first. The amazing fact about the Christian race is that *everyone* who crosses the finishing line is a winner and receives the prize!

And what is the prize? In a physical race today, it might be a medal or trophy, money, or material gift; in Greek and Roman times, winners would receive a wreath of laurel leaves, and the accolade of the crowds of cheering spectators. For me personally, my prize is the sense of achievement when one of my goals has been attained; also, the satisfaction of feeling that I am a now a 'runner' certainly makes all the effort worthwhile.

As Christians, what is our spiritual prize? The apostle Paul tells us that 'Every athlete exercises self-control in all things. They do it to receive a perishable wreath, but we an imperishable' (1 Corinthians 9:25).

Writing to the Philippians, he says, 'I press on toward the goal for the prize of the upward call of God in Christ Jesus' (Philippians 3:14).

Nearing the end of his earthly life, Paul was able to state: 'I have finished the race, I have kept the faith. Henceforth there is laid up for me the crown of righteousness, which the Lord, the righteous judge, will award to me on that day' (2 Timothy 4:7–8). The end of our race as Christians is, of course, when we die. When he penned these words, the apostle knew that, for him, death was imminent, but he was confident of gaining the prize.

In the book of Revelation, written by the apostle John, the Lord Jesus Christ himself addresses seven churches, each with their own particular spiritual issues. To each of these churches He gives a unique promise for those who conquer, to motivate and encourage them to faithful endurance. One such promise states: 'Be faithful unto death, and I will give you the *crown of life*' (Revelation 2:10).

Jesus also prayed for us: 'Father, I desire that they also, whom you have given me, may be *with me* where I am, to see my glory' (John 17:24).

These verses tell us that, for those who finish the Christian race, the prize or crown is eternal glory—it is to be *with Christ*, forever. This is our inheritance, 'imperishable, undefiled, and unfading, kept in heaven for you' (1 Peter 1:4).

Jesus, dying on the cross, told the repentant thief beside Him: 'Today, you will be *with me* in paradise' (Luke 23:43). Jesus has gone to prepare a place for us, so that we can be with Him for ever after we leave this earthly life.

Surely, it is the desire of every true believer to see Jesus face to face, to be made like Him, and to be with Him and enjoy His presence for all eternity. This must be the greatest motivation for us, in all of our struggles in the race—on that great day, it will be worth it all.

When all my labours and trials are o'er,
And I am safe on that beautiful shore,
Just to be near the dear Lord I adore
Will through the ages be glory for me.

O that will be glory for me,
Glory for me, glory for me!
When by His grace I shall look on His face,
That will be glory, be glory for me.

When, by the gift of His infinite grace
I am accorded in heaven a place,
Just to be there and to look on His face
Will through the ages be glory for me.

Friends will be there I have loved long ago;
Joy like a river around me will flow;
Yet just a smile from my Saviour, I know,
Will through the ages be glory for me.
(Chas H. Gabriel, 1856–1932)

3 Partners

O n 18 September 2016, a final race in the World Triathlon series was taking place in Cozumel, Mexico. The competitors had completed the gruelling 1500 metres swim, followed by a 40km cycle ride, and were coming towards the end of the third part of the course, the 10km run. With less than 400 metres to go and the finish line in their sights, Jonny Brownlee was in the lead, with his older brother Alistair and Henry Schoeman, a South African athlete, in second and third place a short distance behind. Suddenly, as Alistair looked ahead, he noticed his brother's legs begin to wobble as fatigue began to overwhelm his body. Jonny slowed down and staggered uncontrollably as his legs gave way underneath him. Alistair and the South African quickly caught up with Jonny and were about to pass him. However, without hesitation, Alistair stretched out his hand to Jonny, grabbed his brother's arm and threw it over his own shoulders, thus supporting Jonny's body weight. The two of them ran together slowly but steadily towards the finish line. A metre before the line, Alistair gently pushed Jonny towards the tape, the impetus causing him to fall over the line and finish in second place, ahead of his gallant older brother in third place. Meanwhile, Henry Schoeman had streaked past them both and won the race, while Alistair had selflessly given up his chance of winning for the sake of Jonny.

While this incident may be considered a somewhat dramatic instance of an athlete assisting a fellow runner, it reminds us that even the more mundane day-to-day support that a running partner can give may be of great significance. Running on your own is at times a lonely business, particularly when first starting out. It can be a great help to find a like-minded person to run with—perhaps a family member or friend—to encourage you and keep you going when you feel like stopping or giving up. Such partners can spur each other on, give helpful advice if one has had more running experience than the other, and provide emotional support when injury strikes

or progress is slow. When I took up running a year ago, I was thankful to have my husband, Michael, join me in attempting the challenge. We have progressed at different rates and have both experienced episodes of injury or illness at various points over the past twelve months, but we still go for most of our runs together and have been able to encourage and support each other to persevere.

Even if you have no one to physically run beside you in every training session you undertake, becoming part of a running group or community can be of tremendous help. This could take the form of joining a local weekly *Parkrun*; running alongside the same people each Saturday morning can be a fun and motivational way of improving performance. Others may become members of an online running community, exchanging advice and providing mutual support, comparing successes (and at times failures). This has been of particular help to me personally during 2020/21, when the world was living with the effects of a global viral pandemic and the consequent 'social distancing' and cancelling of most organised group-running events. Being able to message other like-minded beginner or returning runners and share experiences with them has inspired and challenged me; likewise, I hope that I have been of some help to others also.

Every individual Christian is required to run their own race, but God never intended us to run alone all the way. God has given us local churches—groups of like-minded believers with whom we can meet regularly for worship, teaching and fellowship. The Bible describes these local groups of Christians as being members of a body, or part of a family; we all need each other to enable us to keep spiritually healthy, and to make progress in our race.

Hebrews 10:24–25 exhorts us: 'Let us consider how to stir up one another to love and good works, not neglecting to meet together, as is the habit of some, but encouraging one another, and all the more as you see the Day drawing near.' It is vitally important that once we have become a Christian we seek to join a local church, regularly attend all the meetings and be part of the life of the church. As mentioned in these verses in Hebrews, this is needful both for our own benefit—being spiritually fed and encouraged—and also so that we may be a help and support to others. If God has made this provision for us, how sad it is to see some believers struggling to persevere because they are ignoring this means of mutual encouragement.

In addition to the regular weekly meetings and services that may be held in a local church, there is also the informal, one-to-one contact with individual members of the church, or other Christian friends, which I have found to be of great mutual benefit. Keeping in touch with other believers by visiting them or inviting them to our home, phone calls, text messages or a card to let them know that they are in our thoughts and prayers—these and many others are ways of showing love and support to our brothers and sisters in Christ. We are told in Philippians 2:4: 'Let each of you look not only to his own interests, but also to the interests of others.' When we see another believer struggling, we can put a *spiritual arm* around them and help them towards the finishing line. This may, on occasions, mean offering practical support by the giving of our time, finances or material possessions. Looking out for one another is an integral part of our Christian walk and witness.

Proverbs 17:17 states: 'A friend loves at all times, and a brother is born for adversity.' Speaking from my own experience, I can testify that genuine Christian friendship is a wonderful thing.

A thought for any of you reading these words who are alone, and perhaps not in a position to experience such fellowship with other believers at the present time: remember that 'There is a Friend who sticks closer than a brother' (Proverbs 18:24).

The Lord Jesus promised to His disciples, 'I am with you always, to the end of the age' (Matthew 28:20).

Even on our own, we are never truly alone.

> Blest be the tie that binds
> Our hearts in Christian love;
> The fellowship of kindred minds
> Is like to that above.
>
> Before our Father's throne
> We pour our ardent prayers;
> Our fears, our hopes, our aims are one,
> Our comforts and our cares.

We share our mutual woes,

Our mutual burdens bear;

And often for each other flows

The sympathizing tear.

(John Fawcett, 1740–1817).

'Bear one another's burdens, and so fulfil the law of Christ'
(Galatians 6:2).

4 Progress or perfection?

You may have seen posters, or T-shirts emblazoned with the words: *The goal is progress, not perfection!*
My initial reaction when I recently first read this slogan was to dismiss it as a totally false, thoroughly worldly principle.

> We are God's children now, and what we will be has not yet appeared; but we know that when he [Christ] appears we shall be like him, because we shall see him as he is. And everyone who thus hopes in him purifies himself even as he is pure (1 John 3:2–3).

> Those whom he foreknew he also predestined to be conformed to the image of his Son (Romans 8:29).

> Our citizenship is in heaven, and from it we await a Saviour, the Lord Jesus Christ, who will transform our lowly body to be like his glorious body (Philippians 3:20–21).

We will not only *see* Christ and be with Him forever after we die, but we will also be made *like* Him! Any remaining sin will be removed and we will be made incorruptible, no longer having any desire to sin or ability to sin. We will be truly perfect, like Christ himself.

The apostle Paul, in his letters, often prays for those in the churches to whom he writes. His prayers frequently include such sentiments:

> It is my prayer that ... you may approve what is excellent, and so

be pure and blameless for the day of Christ, filled with the fruit of righteousness that comes through Jesus Christ (Philippians 1:9–11).

He prays for the Ephesian believers, 'That Christ may dwell in your hearts through faith ... that you may be filled with all the fullness of God' (Ephesians 3:17, 19).

In these verses from God's Word, we are clearly told that, as believers, our aim is to become more and more like Jesus Christ. God chose us to be conformed to the image of His Son. He is currently working in us towards this end, and we also are exhorted on our part to strive for that purity and holiness of which Christ is our perfect role-model. We know that one day, after we die and go to be with Christ, that work in us will finally be completed. When He returns and we see Him face to face, we shall have new, resurrection bodies, and *we shall be like Him*—what a glorious prospect! In this sense, our goal is most definitely perfection, not simply some small degree of progress or improvement. And God has guaranteed the completion of our perfection on that day. We should never settle for mediocrity, half-heartedness or second-best in our Christian race; we press on toward the goal; we run in such a way as to obtain the prize.

But, as I considered further the idea of progress versus perfection, I began to see that it was in fact possible to aim for both progress *and* perfection; the two concepts are not mutually exclusive.

How does this work in practice? If you are at all like me, there will be times in your Christian life when, contemplating your final goal of ultimate perfection and of being like Christ, you look at your own shortcomings and failures and see how far short you still fall of God's holy standards. The goal of perfection appears very far off, almost unobtainable, and you may become discouraged and lose hope of ever finishing your 'course with joy' (Acts 20:24). It is in such a situation that the concept of progress rather than perfection may actually be a help, rather than a hindrance to us.

Consider my regular morning run, which is usually over a distance of between 3 and 5 kilometres. On occasions, particularly on days when I decide to run 5km or further, the prospect of completing the distance can be daunting, especially if, after only a few minutes of running, I am already feeling fatigued or struggling to control my breathing. At such times, the temptation is to slow down to a walk, cut the run short, or even give up completely. How can I resist this

thought, and motivate myself to keep going? Definitely not by focusing on the fact that I still have more than 4km left to run! The finishing line can seem a very long way off.

The usual route of my run takes me along the towpath of our local canal. On this section of the canal there are a number of bridges traversing the water, under which the path takes me. I know that to complete a 5km run I need to pass four of these bridges, and that when I reach the fifth, I will have attained the halfway point, at which I am able to turn around and start the *home run*. By mentally dividing my route into these smaller distances and encouraging myself to aim towards the next bridge rather than the distant finishing line, I find that I am enabled to ultimately achieve my final goal.

In a similar way, it can be helpful in our spiritual race to think about making progress each day, rather than hoping for instant perfection, while at the same time not losing sight of our ultimate goal of becoming like Christ. Our Christian race can be broken down into shorter daily runs which, when added together, will eventually make up our complete course 'set before us'.

When we get out of bed each morning and consider the day that lies before us, we do not imagine that by the end of that day we will have attained perfection. But we *do* seek to make progress towards that goal, on a daily basis. At the beginning of each day, let us study God's word and seek His face in prayer, and so be strengthened to be obedient to God's will for us that day, and to become more Christ-like by His grace. God has promised us that 'As your days, so shall your strength be' (Deuteronomy 33:25). As we wait upon the Lord, I can testify, we are given daily strength for our daily needs (Isaiah 40:31). God does not give us the enabling to complete the next week, month or year of our race all at once. In the wilderness, the Israelites had to collect the manna each morning; it would not keep for the following day. In the same way, we need to come not only *boldly*, but *daily*, to the throne of grace to receive help in times of need. If we do this, we will find that by the end of each day, by God's grace, we have 'reached the next bridge'. Or put another way, as James Montgomery (1771–1854) expressed it in his hymn, 'Forever with the Lord', we will be 'a day's march nearer home'.

> Forth in Thy name, O Lord, I go,
> My daily labour to pursue,
> Thee, only Thee, resolved to know
> In all I think, or speak, or do.

Chapter 4

The task Thy wisdom has assigned
O let me cheerfully fulfil,
In all my works Thy presence find,
And prove Thy good and perfect will.

Thee may I set at my right hand,
Whose eyes my inmost substance see,
And labour on at Thy command,
And offer all my works to Thee.

Give me to bear Thy easy yoke,
And every moment watch and pray,
And still to things eternal look,
And hasten to Thy glorious day;

For Thee delightfully employ
Whate'er Thy bounteous grace hath given,
And run my course with even joy,
And closely walk with Thee to heaven.
(Charles Wesley, 1707–88).

5 Predecessors

In considering motivation and inspiration, both to take up running in the first place and also to persevere as a runner, there are plenty of examples of past runners who have been an inspiration to many.

These may include famous Olympic athletes such as the great Emil Zatopek, a Czechoslovakian long-distance runner who won 3 gold medals at the 1952 Helsinki Olympic games. He won both the 5,000 and 10,000 metres events in Helsinki, and then decided at the last minute to enter for the marathon—a distance at which he had never previously competed. To everyone's amazement, he not only won the race, but did so in such a relaxed, easy style, convincingly beating British world record holder, Jim Peters, who was unable to cope with Emil's sustained pace. Zatopek went on to set a total of eighteen world records in long-distance running in addition to his five Olympic gold medals and is considered by many to be one of the greatest runners of all time. He is credited with saying, 'An athlete cannot run with money in his pockets. He must run with hope in his heart and dreams in his head.'[1]

Joanne Pavey is a British athlete who represented Team GB in every Olympic games from 2000 to 2016. While not quite achieving the heights of Zatopek in terms of gold medals and world records, her commitment and endurance in running are a source of inspiration for many. In 2012, she won a 10,000 metres silver medal in the European Championships, and twice she has won medals in the Commonwealth games 5000 metres, with a silver medal in 2006 and a bronze in 2014. Also in 2014, she won the 10,000 metres gold medal at the European championships in Zurich, only ten months after giving birth to her second child. This feat made her the oldest female European champion in athletic history, just a few weeks before her forty-first birthday. It is my understanding that she is currently still in training at the age of forty-six, with the hope of competing in a sixth Olympic games. Her main reason that she continues in her sporting career is that she, in her own words, just 'loves to run.'[2]

As someone who has started running in my early sixties, I was fascinated to learn of an American man called Bob Anderson—a runner, photographer, publisher and film producer. He is well known to many as the founder of the magazine, *Runners World*. Bob commenced running at the age of fourteen, and in 2012 he celebrated fifty years in the sport. By this time, he was sixty-four years old, and decided to mark the achievement by completing fifty races in a year, at an average pace for each race of less than seven minutes per mile. His progress throughout that twelve months was recorded and has been compiled to produce a film entitled *The Long Run*. Watching another person of similar age to myself perform such a feat of speed and endurance, despite injuries and other setbacks, was truly inspirational.

These athletes' stories are relevant to us as Christians, because in the spiritual realm God has also provided us with many people from Bible history who are a great example to us. The author of the book of Hebrews describes them as 'a cloud of witnesses':

> Since we are surrounded by so great a cloud of witnesses, let us...run
> with endurance the race that is set before us (Hebrews 12:1).

This verse is referring back to the previous chapter of Hebrews, which gives details of these witnesses, or *heroes of the faith*, as they have become known. Quite a few are specifically mentioned by name: Abel, Noah, Abraham, Sarah, Isaac, Jacob, Moses etc.; others are grouped together anonymously, simply remembered for their various acts of faith. We are given these examples from the Old Testament not to cause us to despair, feeling that we could never attain the same spiritual heights that they reached, but rather to encourage us in our faith. They serve as examples of ordinary, weak people whom God enabled to persevere, through faith. These *heroes of faith* are painted, like Oliver Cromwell requested, 'warts and all'. We see their flaws and shortcomings as well as their successes, and so can identify with them as we struggle along our own path to heaven. The prophet Elijah is described in the book of James as 'a man with a nature like ours' (James 5:17), to show us that we too can be people whose prayers make a difference. The study of Old Testament believers can be an amazing source of challenge and encouragement to us, and we can learn much from their failures and victories. In addition, we can also gain much from looking at the lives of New Testament disciples like Peter and John, Paul, Priscilla and Aquila, and a host of others. Hebrews 12:1 tells us that *since* (or *because*) we are surrounded by so great a cloud of witnesses, having seen their testimony of how through faith they endured, we should be spurred on to run *our* race with the same endurance. We have the same God, who will strengthen us and keep us as He did those saints of old.

We could point to many other spiritual giants, who have lived since the Bible was penned: Polycarp, Augustine, Wycliffe, Calvin, Tyndale, Luther, Whitfield and Spurgeon, to name a few. Reading biographies of such men as these, or of missionaries like Henry Martin, John Paton, Jim Elliot and Amy Carmichael can be a helpful means of inspiring our faith and resolve to press on towards the goal.

Nearer to home, we can probably all think of people who have been a help to us in our spiritual pilgrimage: pastors and church leaders, Sunday school teachers, faithful friends. Not least of these, we should not forget that, for those of us who have had the privilege of growing up in a Christian home, our own godly parents have no doubt been a

great blessing and encouragement to us. I am thankful to have been among that number. My parents were not without their failings, but I am still able to look back on their lives and see how they sought to live out their faith. My mother, in particular, left a legacy of good works performed out of love for her Saviour. I can recall the children she regularly fostered; the troubled teenagers she and my father cared for (often at great personal cost); the befriending of an old lady who lived in squalor with her numerous cats as her only company—taking her meals, doing her washing, and inviting her to share Christmas Day with our family. Despite often suffering from illness herself, my mother was always looking to the needs of others. I recall her regularly writing letters to me, while I was at university, keeping me updated on news from home, and seeking to encourage me in my faith. She once sent me some words from a hymn, which said:

> I do not ask, O Lord, that all my life should be
> An easy, smooth or pleasant path, t'would not be good for me;

But O, I ask, dear Lord, that grace and strength be given
To keep me fighting all the way that leads to God and heaven.
(Fannie Jolliffe, 1862–1943)[3]

These are but a few instances of how my mother set me an example of love in action, as well as always seeking to tell others of the love of Christ.

Let us therefore consider the example of 'so great a cloud of witnesses', both those ancient and those more recent, 'so that you may not be sluggish, but imitators of those who through faith and patience inherit the promises' (Hebrews 6:12).

For all the saints, who from their labours rest,
Who Thee by faith before the world confessed,
Thy name, O Jesus, be for ever blessed,
Hallelujah! Hallelujah!

Thou wast their Rock, their Fortress and their Might;
Thou, Lord, their Captain in the well-fought fight;
Thou, in the darkness drear, their one true Light,
Hallelujah! Hallelujah!

O may Thy soldiers, faithful, true, and bold,
Fight as the saints, who nobly fought of old,
And win, with them, the victor's crown of gold.
Hallelujah! Hallelujah!
(William Walsham How, 1823–1897)

 6 Prototype

However inspirational a particular athlete may have been, they can never be a perfect example to us of how to run. Whether it be Mo Farah, Sebastian Coe, or the great 400 metre runner, Michael Johnson, they have all had their 'off days', and none of them were invincible. We can certainly learn much from them, but we should not put them on such a pedestal that we are unable to see their failings.

When I was working in General Practice, one of my older female patients came to see me one morning with a history of chest pains. Her description of her symptoms was a little vague, but after further questioning and examination, I decided to refer her to a heart specialist for investigation. She was duly seen by the consultant, and after various tests a diagnosis of severe coronary artery disease was made. She subsequently underwent coronary artery bypass surgery, which relieved her symptoms. Whenever this lady saw me after this, either in the surgery or while shopping in town, she always greeted me with the words, 'Doctor Worsell, you saved my life!', and sang my praises to all her friends. She was extremely grateful to me for referring her to the cardiologist, and in her eyes, I could do no wrong. But this was obviously not a totally realistic assessment: even though I sought to be a good, caring doctor, I was not infallible.

Although many of the saints referred to in the last chapter

provided a good spiritual example to follow, they all had one thing in common: they were none of them without their faults. They were all *sinners saved by grace*. If only we could have just one example to inspire us who was perfect, without sin, who never yielded to temptation—and that, of course, is what we do indeed have, in the Person of the Lord Jesus Christ! The verse that has already been quoted more than once, Hebrews 12:1, continues with these words from verse 2: 'Let us run with endurance the race that is set before us, *looking to Jesus*, the founder and perfector of our faith ...' Jesus is our perfect example, or *prototype*. (While a prototype can be an early sample or model of a product which is then tested and may be improved upon, when referring to a person the word prototype can be used to mean someone who was the first, or typical one who serves as a model or inspiration for those who come later). Jesus is described in Hebrews as our 'forerunner', the One who has gone before us into heaven itself:

> We have this as a sure and steadfast anchor of the soul, a hope that enters into the inner place behind the curtain, where Jesus has gone as a *forerunner* on our behalf, having become a high priest forever after the order of Melchizedek (Hebrews 6:19–20).

The Lord Jesus Christ has not only run the race ahead of us, giving us a perfect example to follow, but through his life, death and resurrection He has accomplished certain things *on our behalf*, without which we could never have any hope of reaching heaven. We can only be sure of going to heaven because Jesus has gone before us, because He has already offered the perfect sacrifice that opens the door for us. We can only be sure of arriving there safely because Jesus has become our great High Priest, who always lives to intercede for us. He has become a priest 'after the order of Melchizedek'—that is a priest forever—pleading His own blood before the Father's throne on our behalf, and thus securing an eternal redemption for us.

And so, in Hebrews 12:1, we are now told to run with endurance... 'looking to Jesus'. What does this mean for us in practical terms—how and why are we to 'look to Jesus'? I would like to suggest three reasons:

- Because He is the founder and perfecter of our faith. He is the One who has made it possible for us to be in the spiritual race, the One who will ensure that we finish the race, and the One on whom our faith depends from beginning to end. As we continue to run day by day, we can meditate on this truth and be strengthened to keep going, even when the going gets tough. Christ has done everything necessary to purchase our salvation by His death on the cross, by paying the price for all our sin and bringing us back to God. He has promised to give us grace and strength for each day of our journey, however long or short our path may be. He has gone ahead of us into heaven and will make certain that each one of His people will also make it safely to the same destination, to be with Him forever. The security of our past, present and future, in and through Jesus Christ, should help us to 'strengthen ... [our] weak knees, and make straight paths for our feet, so that what is lame may not be put out of joint but rather be healed' (Hebrews 12:12–13).
- Because Jesus has set us the perfect example of endurance.

We are told that, 'For the joy that was set before him [Jesus] endured the cross, despising the shame, and is seated at the right hand of the throne of God' (Hebrews 12:2). The following verse (v. 3) encourages us to 'Consider him who endured from sinners such hostility against himself, so that you may not grow weary or fainthearted.' Suffering and trials are all part of the Christian life and show that God loves us and is treating us as sons. Hebrews 12:6 reminds us that 'the Lord disciplines the one he loves', and although such training and discipline is not pleasant when we are going through it, it will produce the fruit of righteousness in our character if we submit to God's dealings with us, which are always for our ultimate good. As in training for a 10K or marathon, hard work and discipline is required, so too in our Christian race, trials and tribulations are part of God's training, so that we may share His holiness. When I was twenty-two years old and just commencing my final year at Medical School, my mother suffered a severe brain haemorrhage (stroke) and died in hospital three days later. This was a devastating experience for me, and while my faith in God did not waver, I struggled to understand the reason why God should take my mother 'home' at the age of fifty-two. Trying to keep going with my academic studies through my grief required much sustaining grace from the Lord. Looking back forty years later, I still have not found all the answers to my questions, but I am learning to trust that God loves me and always does what is good in His sight—He does not owe me any explanations. Through all of our struggles, we can take heart by considering what Jesus endured during His time on this earth, which was far worse than anything we will ever have to experience. He endured 'death, even death on a cross' (Philippians 2:8); surely His supreme example should spur us on in our own race.

- Because Jesus has gone ahead of us into heaven and is there preparing a place for us. We can look to Him, fix our eyes on Him, knowing that we are heading in that same direction, to the same destination, and that when we arrive, He will be there to welcome us home! As we run towards the goal, this hope should inspire us to do so with perseverance, looking at the One who loved us and gave Himself for us. At times, our earthly view of Jesus may be faint or dim, and we may almost lose sight of our Saviour when passing through severe trials. But, like Peter attempting to walk on the water towards Jesus, if we look at Jesus rather than on the waves threatening to engulf us, we can know His presence and strength. As we go on in our race, the nearer we get to the finishing line, the clearer the view of Christ we should have. As we grow older, let us meditate more and more on our Saviour each day, until that day when our faith becomes sight. Then we will see His face and worship Him forever. Let us not grow weary when we have such a glorious hope!

May the mind of Christ my Saviour
Live in me from day to day,
By His love and power controlling
All I do and say.

May I run the race before me,
Strong and brave to face the foe,
Looking only unto Jesus
As I onward go.
(Kate Barclay Wilkinson, 1859–1928)

7 Power

The food that you eat can be important when taking running seriously. Both the regular daily diet, plus the actual amount, type and timing of food and fluid intake in the hours before a race, are nowadays considered to play a vital role in ensuring that an athlete is able to perform at their optimal level. Today, there is a whole industry focused on 'fuelling your run', and a professional runner will almost certainly have their own nutritionist to advise them.

Even if we are simply running for pleasure and to improve our fitness a little, our progress will probably be hindered if we exist on a diet of pizzas, chips and cream cakes. It makes sense to try and eat a reasonably healthy diet containing plenty of fruit, vegetables, protein, vitamins and minerals, and to cut down on the less healthy options full of sugar and fat. For the actual day of a run, there is also plenty of advice available in books or online about exactly what to have for breakfast; how many hours before the race it should be eaten; which fluids to drink etc. A few years ago, the popular running magazine *Runner's World* produced a list of what they called the 'Eight commandments of good running nutrition'[1]:

- Plan your diet (regular healthy eating).
- Eat little and often.
- Don't ignore the main meals.
- Ensure sufficient supplements (vitamins and minerals).

- Drink more water.
- Don't forget your pre-race meal (don't skip breakfast!).
- Learn to drink on the run (for longer races).
- Eat for recovery (after your run).

We can see from this that both a regular healthy diet and a race-day eating plan are very important in ensuring sufficient energy being available for our bodies to run well.

Thinking in spiritual terms, what is the source of the power or energy to run our Christian race; from where can we obtain it? The Christian life is not turning over a new leaf, or a set of rules that we try hard to keep, summoning up all our own resources of strength to do so. It is a new life, given to us by God when we turn to Him in repentance and faith. The Bible describes it as being 'born again' (John 3:7), or 'born of the Spirit' (John 3:6). An integral part of this new birth is God's Holy Spirit coming to live within us; in fact, a person cannot be a real Christian without this indwelling of the Holy Spirit:

> Anyone who does not have the Spirit of Christ does not belong to him (Romans 8:9).

But do we then automatically have the strength that we need for every task each day, because we have the Spirit within us? If not, what is the secret?

I believe that there are three interlinked strands that are all necessary in order to know God's power at work in our lives, day by day: God's presence, God's promises and prayer.

It is impossible to separate these three strands, because God has ordained that they should all work together in such a way that we cannot experience His strength when any one of them is missing. Our strength comes from Christ, by His Spirit, but we receive this strength through prayer, through daily communion with Christ, and by reading and meditating on what He says to us in his precious Word.

1. God's Presence

It is true: we do have the Holy Spirit within us if we are a real Christian, but it is still possible to know His presence and empowering to a greater or lesser degree. We are told not to grieve or to quench the Spirit (Ephesians 4:30; 1 Thessalonians 5:19); in contrast, we are exhorted to be 'filled with the Spirit', to walk in the Spirit, to 'set our mind[s] on the Spirit' and be 'led by the Spirit' (Ephesians 5:18; Galatians 5:16, 18; Romans 8:6, 14). Jesus himself, when teaching His disciples about prayer, told them to ask, seek and knock, and assured them that if we, who are evil, know how to give good gifts to our children, 'how much more will the heavenly Father give the Holy Spirit to those who ask him!' (Luke 11:9–13). It seems therefore, that God wants us to come to Him in prayer, recognizing our own weakness, and to cry out to Him for more of His Holy Spirit's presence and power in our lives, day by day. On another occasion, Jesus reminded His disciples that they needed to 'abide in Him', as the branches of a vine need to be joined to the vine in order to bear fruit, because without Him they could do nothing (John 15:4–5). The apostle Paul prayed that the Ephesian believers would be 'strengthened with power through his Spirit in your inner being' (Ephesians 3:16); he wanted them to know this more and more, until they were 'filled with all the fullness of God' (v. 19).

2. God's Promises

To be spiritually strong and healthy, we need a regular daily diet that includes reading and meditating on God's Word, the Bible, so that we receive the spiritual food—the energy—for each day. 'All Scripture is breathed out by God and profitable for teaching, for reproof, for correction, and for training in righteousness, that the man of God may be complete, equipped for every good work' (2 Tim. 3:16–17). God has given us His 'precious and very great promises' (2 Peter 1:4); by studying the many promises in the Bible, we can be encouraged and strengthened:

> As your days, so shall your strength be (Deuteronomy 33:25).

> My grace is sufficient for you, for my strength is made perfect in weakness (2 Cor 12:9, NKJV).

> They who wait for the Lord shall renew their strength … they shall run and not be weary (Isaiah 40:31).

> Fear not, for I am with you … I will strengthen you, I will help you (Isaiah 41:10).

> Cast your burden on the Lord and he will sustain you (Psalm 55:22).

These, and so many more promises can help us to 'lift [our] … drooping hands and strengthen [our] … weak knees' (Hebrews 12:12). Some people have found it helpful to keep a notebook in which to write down any promises of God that they come across in their daily searching of the Scriptures, and which they can refer back to in times of need. I have also attempted to keep such a journal on and off over the years, where I jot down a few thoughts from the Bible passage in my daily reading, and any specific verses, that have particularly struck me. I do not manage to keep it up every single day, but when I have done so, it has been a means of encouragement to my own soul.

Chapter 7

God has promised us so much: forgiveness and cleansing from all our sins; strength for each day of our race here on earth; the assurance that He will complete the work which He has begun in us; and an eternal home with Him after our course here is finished. What an amazing God we have! But we should remember that, while one specific verse may come to mind and provide strength at a particular moment of need, it is the regular, personal study of the whole of God's Word that needs to be our main source of spiritual fuel, so that our tank is never running on empty. Our pastor recently told us of his experience as a teenager, running a marathon for the first time. One of the mistakes that he made was to skip breakfast on the morning of the race. Having started off well, when he reached about the twenty mile point, he suddenly 'hit the wall', realizing that all of his available energy had been used up; needless to say, he found the last six miles extremely difficult and painful! In a similar way, it is vital that we feed on God's Word each day (preferably at the beginning of the day), so that we have the strength and resources for whatever lies in store for us in the succeeding hours.

3. Prayer

I find that it is one of the mysteries of prayer, that although God knows everything, including all of our individual needs, He still wants us to pray and ask Him to supply those needs. In what we call the Lord's Prayer, Jesus taught His disciples how to pray; one of the requests in this prayer is 'Give us this day our daily bread' (Matthew 6:11). And so, He encourages us to ask for our daily needs to be provided. Even though God has promised us many things (including spiritual strength) in His Word, it is still necessary for us to frequently pray and cry out to God to give us this enabling.

CH Spurgeon, in his commentary on Psalm 121, with its promise that God 'will not let your foot be moved' (v. 3), says this: 'Promised preservation should be the subject of perpetual prayer. We pray and believe. Those who have God for their Keeper will be safe from all the perils of the way.'[2] God's promises should lead us to utter heartfelt pleas to Him for those promises to be fulfilled in our daily experience.

Many of David's Psalms are in fact just that—he is crying out to God for help and strength in his various trials. For instance, in Psalm 61, he says 'Hear my cry, O God, listen to my prayer; ... lead me to the rock that is higher than I' (vv. 1–2). We should follow David's example, and also that of the apostles in Acts 4, who prayed for God's enabling to continue speaking His Word with boldness (v. 29).

Even the Lord Jesus, while here on earth, spent much time in prayer to His heavenly Father. Communion with God the Father in prayer, and dependence upon the presence and power of the Holy Spirit were part of His sharing in our humanity, albeit without sin. If Jesus needed to pray, how much more do we? 'Let us then with confidence draw near to the throne of grace, that we may receive mercy and find grace to help in time of need' (Hebrews 4:16).

> Have you not known? Have you not heard? The LORD is the everlasting God, the Creator of the ends of the earth. He does not faint or grow weary; his understanding is unsearchable. He gives power to the faint, and to him who has no might he increases strength. Even youths shall faint and be weary, and young men shall fall exhausted; but they who wait for the LORD shall renew their

strength; they shall mount up with wings like eagles; they shall run and not be weary; they shall walk and not faint. (Isaiah 40:28–31)

 # 8 Problems

There is one aspect of running that I feel it would be wrong to gloss over or neglect, and that is the failures and setbacks in our running experience. These may, in some instances, be due to illness or circumstances beyond our control which lead to our being physically unable to run for a period of time. However, I want in this chapter to focus on those falls or injuries we sustain, that are at least partially of our own making, and which we could perhaps have prevented. Thinking back to my initial attempts to start running, there are two particular examples of this that spring to mind.

The first occurred when I was only at the stage of considering the possibility of attempting to run and had not begun any specific running programme. My ten-year-old granddaughter had taken up running a few weeks earlier and wanted to go for a short run while staying at our house, so I offered to walk behind her and keep an eye on her as she did so. As we started off down the road, I just thought that I would try to jog slowly for the first minute or two, so that I would not fall very far behind her. After about forty metres of running, I suddenly felt a twinge of pain in my left side, causing me to stop running and revert to walking. This pain persisted as I continued walking, and I realized that I had pulled a muscle. I was amazed that it had happened so easily, with so little exertion, and that it subsequently prevented me from starting a running programme for several weeks until it had healed.

The second instance happened shortly after beginning the *Couch to 5K* programme. I had more or less recovered from the pulled muscle in my left side a few weeks earlier and was on the second week of the course—just at the stage of alternate running and walking for between one and two minutes at a time for a total of twenty minutes. Running around our local reservoir on a crisp February morning, I began to sense a slight discomfort in my right knee. This eased off as I walked but recurred as soon as I attempted to run again, and gradually increased in intensity with each ninety second run. Frustrated, I was forced to complete the course at a slow limp and was later diagnosed as having strained my medial cruciate ligament. Several weeks of pain

and visits to a physiotherapist ensued before my knee was sufficiently strong enough to restart training.

Both these injuries that I sustained were largely due to my lack of preparation. In the first situation, I was foolish to imagine that I could just start to run, especially at my age and with CFS, without any prior practice or warm-up. I should have waited until I had read the available advice and started on the official course, beginning very gradually. The second injury might have been prevented if I had undertaken regular exercises to improve my strength and mobility, in conjunction with my running programme. These types of exercises are specifically designed to reduce the risk of injury by strengthening the relevant muscles used in running; I later changed to a different beginners' running programme which included these types of exercises as an integral part of the training and have thankfully been injury-free since that time.

As well as the type of injuries I have just described, *falls* are also a significant risk while running. These may be due to tripping over an obstacle on the path, bumping into something (or someone), slipping on a patch of icy ground, or simply tripping over your own feet. Sometimes no actual injury is sustained, apart from to one's pride, whereas on other occasions there may be significant cuts, bruises or even broken bones. Of the prolific advice that has been offered to try and help prevent such falls, the main tips appear to be:

Look where you are going! Don't run with your head down, looking at your feet, but look up, a short distance ahead, watching out for any obstacles or uneven surfaces.

Focus. Concentrate on what you are doing. Preferably do not wear headphones while running or let yourself get distracted.

Pick your feet up. You are more likely to trip over your feet if you do not lift your feet and ankles high enough when running. Also, make sure your shoelaces are tied properly, with no loose ends dangling.

Use the right shoes. If running on trails—hilly or uneven surfaces—wear trail shoes for extra stability, and spikes for icy conditions. Check your running gait and ensure that the shoes you buy are suited to your gait; wear orthotic insoles if necessary. Replace your shoes when they become too worn.

Perform regular exercise for core body strength and balance. If our muscles are weak, we are more likely to stumble and fall.

How does this apply to our spiritual race? Because sadly, at whatever stage of the race we are at, *there is a danger of stumbling and falling.*

The Bible tells us clearly 'Therefore let anyone who thinks that he stands take heed lest he fall' (I Corinthians 10:12).

Let us consider some of the reasons why we as Christians may stumble and fall.

1. Pride, and confidence in our own ability is something that we are warned of in Proverbs 16:18: 'Pride goes before destruction, and a haughty spirit before a fall.' The answer to this is to be humble, recognizing our own spiritual weakness and daily reliance on God's strength to run the race. In his book about the life of David, *The Making of a Man of God*, Alan Redpath comments that 'There is never a day in any man's life but that he is dependent upon the grace of God for power and the blood of Jesus for cleansing.'[1] Jesus said, 'apart from me you can do nothing' (John 15:5).

We are given examples of various characters in the Bible for our instruction (1 Corinthians 10:11; Romans 15:4); this includes their falls and failures as well as their successes. King David is one such person, a man who was described as being *after God's own heart* (1 Sam. 13:14; Acts 13:22), yet his sad fall into the sins of adultery and murder should make us realize that none of us are immune from such danger.

'Oh, from what heights of blessing it is possible for a man to fall. To what depths of sin a man can descend, even with all that spiritual background!' (Alan Redpath[2]). Let us remember God's promise that 'as our days so shall our strength be' and look to Him to supply all our needs.

2. Complacency is always a danger, particularly as we grow older, I find. The temptation to take things easy, thinking that we have 'done our bit', and that it is time to let the younger believers do the work. This was part of King David's problem, when as an older man he stayed at home in his palace one springtime—the season when kings normally go out to battle. He sent his troops out with Joab, but he himself decided to rest (2 Samuel 11). It was under these circumstances that he was led astray and ended up committing adultery with Bathsheba, followed by plotting the murder of her husband, Uriah. Let us not forget that we are in a battle, and that we have a powerful enemy, the devil, who is constantly prowling around like a roaring lion 'seeking whom he may devour' (1 Peter 5:8). If we become slack in our spiritual discipline and careless about our regular times of prayer and study of God's Word, we can be easy targets for the devil's attacks. Jesus warned His disciples to 'Watch and pray, that you may not enter into temptation. The spirit indeed is willing but the flesh is weak' (Matthew 26:41). We need to be alert, and on our guard at all times against the world, the flesh and the devil.

Are we taking sin seriously in our lives, or do we consider certain sins as only small and insignificant? Hebrews 12:1 calls us to 'Lay aside *every* weight, and sin which clings so closely', so that we will be able to run with endurance the race set before us. There should be no place for anything in our lives that could hinder our running or cause us to stumble.

3. *Being led astray by our own desires* is also a cause for falling into sin, according to James 1:14. He speaks of friendship with the world as being enmity against God. It is possible for us, almost without realizing it, to become so engrossed with the things of this life that we forget that we are strangers and pilgrims here on earth. We find ourselves thinking like the world, seeking after worldly pleasures and comforts, pursuing our hobbies and ambitions, until we are like

salt that has lost its taste. I find I need to remind myself that even legitimate desires—such as for a happy family life, a comfortable home, and freedom from cares or sickness—are not what I should be aiming for. Paul spoke of a man named Demas, who deserted him because he was 'in love with this present world' (2 Tim. 4:10). When I read of the *heroes of the faith* in Hebrews 11, I can see how their mindset was different from this. Abraham was 'looking forward to the city that has foundations, whose designer and builder is God' (v. 10). He and others 'acknowledged that they were strangers and exiles on the earth' (v. 13). Moses chose 'to be mistreated with the people of God than to enjoy the fleeting pleasures of sin … for he was looking to the reward' (vv. 25–26). We need to remember to fix our eyes on Jesus, knowing that 'the things that are seen are transient, but the things that are unseen are eternal' (2 Corinthians 4:18).

Thankfully, God has provided the resources that we need, in order to enable us to stand rather than fall:

> No temptation has overtaken you that is not common to man. God is faithful, and he will not let you be tempted beyond your ability, but with the temptation he will also provide the way of escape, that you may be able to endure it (1 Corinthians 10:13).

> Now to him who is able to keep you from stumbling and to present you blameless before the presence of his glory with great joy (Jude v. 24).

> My help comes from the LORD … He will not let your foot be moved; he who keeps you will not slumber (Psalm 121:2–3).

God has also given us details of many people in the Bible, like

David, to help us, warn us and instruct us, so that hopefully we will learn from their errors and not yield to similar temptations.

But if, despite all that has been said, we *do* fall, let us consider what our response should be.

Firstly, it is vital to *recognise our condition*. You might think that if we have tripped over and are lying flat on our face, we could hardly miss the fact! And yet, it is possible to be in such a sad spiritual state that we are unaware of it. Samson, when he finally gave in to Delilah's persistence and his hair was shaved off, 'awoke from his sleep and said, "I will go out as at other times and shake myself free." *But he did not know that the LORD had left him'* (Judges 16:20).

The church at Ephesus was told to 'Remember therefore from where you have fallen' (Revelation 2:5). Before we can benefit from the correct treatment, we need to realize that we are injured and that we require help to be healed.

Once we see our condition, the next step is to *repent quickly.* Do not be like David, who persisted in his hard-hearted condition for about a year, allowing his first sin of adultery to lead on to murder, and to a prolonged period of time in which he was not running well spiritually, was feeling miserable and unable to experience the joy of his salvation. The devil is crafty; before we commit a particular sin, he tries to tell us that it is not really a sin—or at least, that it is just a tiny one. Then, if we do sin, he is very keen to make us think that it is such a huge sin that we cannot repent of it, and that God would never forgive us. We think that we have to somehow make ourselves a bit better or leave a period of time before we can come back to God and ask for His forgiveness. But the devil is, and always has been, a liar, and we should not listen to his lies. Instead, we should not delay in turning back to God but come quickly, confessing our sins to Him, and remembering that He is merciful and ready to forgive. Read Psalm 51, written by David after he had been spoken to about his sin by the prophet Nathan, and like him, acknowledge your sin and seek God's cleansing of your heart.

Thirdly, having repented, we need to *be assured of God's forgiveness*. 'If we confess our sins, he [God] is faithful and just to forgive us our sins and to cleanse us from all unrighteousness' (1 John 1:9). God says, 'I am he who blots out your transgressions for my own sake, and I will not remember your sins' (Isaiah 43:25). He removes our sins from us 'as far as the east is from the west' (Psalm 103:12).

1 John 2:1–2 says, 'I am writing these things to you so that you may not sin. But if anyone does sin, we have an advocate with the Father, Jesus Christ the righteous. He is the propitiation for our sins'. Jesus Christ, God's Son, has taken the punishment for *all* your sin on the cross; it has been completely paid for!

> When Satan tempts me to despair,
> And tells me of the guilt within,
> Upward I look, and see Him there
> Who made an end of all my sin.
> (Charitie Lees Bancroft/de Chenez, 1841–1923).

> My sin—O the bliss of that glorious thought!—
> My sin, not in part, but the whole,
> Is nailed to His cross, and I bear it no more:
> Praise the Lord, praise the Lord, O my soul!
> (Horatio Gates Spafford, 1828–1888).

But there is one note of caution, in case we go too far and start thinking that sinning does not matter because God will always forgive us. David's sin was forgiven and his relationship with God was restored, but there were consequences as a result of his sinful behaviour. God told David, through the prophet Nathan, 'The child who is born to you shall die' (2 Samuel 12:14). There were also consequences for his future family life, and things would never be quite the same again: 'a forgiven man may still have to reap what he has sown'.[3] But ultimately, David kept running and finished his race.

> For though a righteous man may fall seven times, he still gets up
> [again] (Proverbs 24:16, *Berean Study Bible*).

Falling and failure is not final; *all* of God's children will make it to heaven, not one shall be lost. By God's grace and daily enabling, we too shall arrive at our destination. And there, we will fall down in a different way—in worship of our wonderful Saviour.

9 Pace

In athletics terms, a person's pace is the distance they cover in a fixed period of time, i.e. their speed. *Pacing*, when referring to running, is the technique of adjusting your speed at different stages of a run, in order to produce the fastest possible time for the total distance run. For running a short distance, such as a 100 metres sprint, pacing is not really required; it is basically about running as fast as you can for a short period of time. For Usain Bolt at his peak, that meant running extremely fast for a little less than ten seconds, while for the rest of the world population that distance would take slightly longer. However, in middle- or long-distance races such as 5km, 10km or a marathon, pacing can play a very important part in determining who wins the race, or whether a new record is set.

Setting off at too fast a pace at the beginning of a race can often lead to running out of steam later on, and either being unable to finish or producing a slower time than expected. It is, therefore, vital to run at a pace that you are comfortable with and that you will be able to sustain for the distance that you are running. That will usually mean that the longer the distance being run, the slower the average pace. However, as a person improves their strength and stamina, they should be able to sustain a slightly faster pace for a longer distance. Most athletes try to keep a little bit of energy in reserve for the last lap, or the end part of the race, and try to put in a final burst of speed towards the finish line.

In top-level athletics, some races may have one or more official *pacemakers*; these are athletes who lead at a set pace for the first section of a middle- or long-distance race, in order to ensure a fast time, and they usually drop out for the latter part of the race. Pacemakers are often employed when a world record is being attempted, but at lower levels most runners do not have this luxury and need to judge for themselves if they are running at the right speed. Learning to pace is a difficult but essential skill for racing faster and improving stamina. It takes time to master.

In comparing the Christian life to a race, one obvious difference is that, unlike a physical race, we do not know how long or short our course will be. This means that, as we think about how we should pace ourselves in an effort to run well spiritually, we face a degree of uncertainty as to how long we will be required to keep running. However, it will probably be true to say that for most of us, our race will not be a sprint. The writer of Hebrews had in mind a longer distance such as a marathon, which he encouraged us to 'run with endurance' (12:1). How then should we pace ourselves?

One thing that is worth considering is that we are not competing against other people in order to beat them and win the prize. As mentioned previously, in this race *all* who complete the course win the prize. In that sense, it is not how fast you run, it's about finishing the race that matters. But in order to do this, we have to progress at a pace that we can sustain (with God's help). It is possible to begin running with great enthusiasm and zeal as a new Christian, only to find that we run out of energy and motivation when the going gets tough. In the Parable of the Sower (Matthew 13), Jesus spoke of the seed that fell on rocky ground. He told His disciples that this was like 'the one who hears the word and immediately receives it with joy, yet he has no root in himself, but endures for a while and when tribulation or persecution arises on account of the word, immediately he falls away' (vv. 20–21). Remember, it is 'the one who endures to the end' (Matt. 24:13) who will be saved, not the one who sets off the fastest.

Anyone who has read the biographies of men such as David Brainerd, missionary to the native American Indians, or Henry Martyn, missionary in India and Persia, cannot fail to be impressed by their zeal for Christ and the amount that they achieved in their relatively short lives. Both of them suffered poor physical health, which was exacerbated by the intensity of their labours on the mission field. Brainerd contracted tuberculosis and died in America in 1747, aged only twenty-nine. Martyn, who was originally inspired to become a missionary by reading of Brainerd's exploits, also suffered with tuberculosis during his time abroad. Having completed his translation of the New Testament into the Persian language, he died in 1812 of a fever (and exhaustion) while attempting the long journey home across Turkey on horseback. He was just thirty-one years old. It is highly likely that had both these men stayed at home rather than become missionaries, or even just taken things at a slightly slower pace and sought the necessary medical attention for their illnesses, they would have survived significantly longer. But is that how we as Christians should view their lives? They gave their all for Christ; like CT Studd, another pioneer missionary, their mindset was encapsulated by the thought that 'If Jesus Christ be God and died for me, then no sacrifice can be too great for me to make for Him.'[1] Similarly, Jim Elliot, famously martyred by the Auca Indians in Ecuador in 1956 along with four fellow missionaries, said 'He is no fool, who gives what he cannot keep, to gain what he cannot lose.'[2] Others have coined the phrase 'better to burn out than rust out', when speaking of our service for the Lord, and Henry Martyn himself is said to have died with the words 'Let me burn out for God'.

I would add a proviso that, as a general rule, it is a good thing to look after our bodies to keep them healthy, by eating the right type and quantity of food, obtaining regular exercise and sufficient sleep, and avoiding harmful substances such as tobacco, drugs or excessive alcohol. Sadly, as a GP, I have seen many examples of the damage that can result from either abusing the body or neglecting its proper care. Some men have needed an amputation of one or more limbs due to the effects of nicotine on their arteries caused by cigarette smoking, and one lady slowly destroyed her body and mind through her alcohol addiction, despite attempts from her family and myself to help her. In a somewhat less extreme but more common means of mistreatment of our bodies, overeating and consequent obesity can also put us at increased risk of various health conditions such as diabetes and heart disease. Our bodies are temples of the Holy Spirit, and we should be disciplined and self-controlled in the way that we treat them. There may be many illnesses or injuries which are beyond our control and which we may still experience in spite of all our efforts to be healthy, but we should seek to avoid conditions which *are* under our control. There needs to be a balance, however, and we should not veer to the opposite extreme and become over-anxious or obsessed with our bodily health and safety, so that, as a consequence, we are hindered or prevented from running the race.

The apostle Paul suffered many things for the sake of Christ. He endured 'far greater labours, far more imprisonments, with countless beatings and often near death. Five times I received...forty lashes less one. Three times I was beaten with rods. Once I was stoned. Three times I was shipwrecked...in toil and hardship, through many a sleepless night, in hunger and thirst, often without food, in cold and exposure' (2 Corinthians 11:23–27). For Paul, to live was Christ, and to die was gain; we too should be willing to suffer anything which God permits or ordains for us as part of our walk with Him, as we labour, 'struggling with all his energy that he powerfully works within me' (Colossians 1:29). Let us seek to know God's will for our lives each day, and by His enabling grace to be obedient to that will each day. That way we will truly be running at the best pace.

Caleb, one of the twelve men whom Moses sent to spy out the land of Canaan, was gifted by God with a long and healthy life. At the age of eighty-five years old he was able to say, 'I am still as strong today as I was in the day that Moses sent me; my strength now is as my strength was then, for war and for going and coming' (Joshua 14:11). God may choose to similarly sustain us physically into old age, and if He does so we should be truly thankful. But, for most of us, this is not the case. As we grow older physically, our bodies tend to gradually slow down and have less energy. We have difficulty sustaining the same level of activity into our sixties and beyond which was normal for us in our twenties and thirties. There is a natural downward progression, pictured in Isaiah 40:31, which describes those who wait for the Lord:

> They who wait for the LORD shall renew their strength; they shall *mount up* with wings like eagles; they shall *run* and not be weary; they shall *walk* and not faint.

We see in this image the young man in full strength almost seeming to soar and fly, followed by the more mature man, still able to run steadily without tiring, and lastly by those in old age, who are glad to be able to simply walk without stumbling. But should we, therefore, slow down spiritually as we age physically, or if we are beset by bodily illness, disease or disability? For some, like myself, chronic sickness may strike in younger years, with conditions such as Chronic Fatigue Syndrome/ME, or some might even suffer from diseases like cystic fibrosis, present from birth, which gradually worsen with age. For such people, many forms of physical activity are impossible, and they may feel of little use spiritually because of their physical limitations. What is running *at a good pace* in terms of our Christian race? Is it defined by how healthy and strong we are, and by the level of our participation in the type of Christian service which demands much physical or mental stamina?

Some of us may have taken part in beach missions, holiday Bible clubs or church evangelistic outreach, particularly in our teens and twenties. I know of young people who have spent almost every week of their school or university summer break helping on one beach mission after another, hardly having time to rest or catch their breath. While we admire those who have both the zeal and the energy to sustain such active service, most of us slightly older Christians need to pace ourselves by undertaking shorter periods of service, with longer intervals between them, in order to persevere and not become physically worn out. However, I do not believe this necessarily means that we are *slowing down* spiritually.

After I started suffering with Chronic Fatigue Syndrome, I initially felt physically unable to participate in any evangelistic activities such as United Beach Missions' week-long outreaches at various seaside resorts in the UK (something which I had previously taken part in when younger and healthier). Having to stand up for long periods in open air meetings or run around playing with children on the beach was beyond me. However, two or three years after my diagnosis of CFS, after discussion with team leaders who understood my limitations but still encouraged me to be involved as I felt able, I booked for one week of mission at Llandudno in July 2005. By this time, I had purchased a mobility scooter which fitted into the boot of my car and used this to transport me up and down the road from the UBM house to the promenade each morning and afternoon. I could also use it to sit down on and rest, if I felt particularly tired at any point during the day's activities or, if necessary, return back to the team accommodation for a break. While certain tasks were difficult due to requiring more energy than I possessed, I was able to take on other roles, such as producing posters and artwork for the mission, and being the treasurer for the week's finances. In this way, I was still enabled to serve the Lord in some capacity, even if not quite the same way as in my younger days, and, by God's grace, I had the opportunity to go on similar missions for several summers after this. Subsequently, over the past ten years, I have become more involved with Christian Answer missions, seeking to share the gospel with people in towns and cities throughout England, Wales and France. These missions usually last between four and seven days, with regular open-air meetings in the city centres. The meetings include preaching by some of the men on the team, and one-to-one conversations with anyone who stops to listen and is willing to talk. More recently, they have also incorporated the use of a book table, stocked with a selection of free evangelistic books and leaflets, and I have really felt that this aspect of the outreach has been suited to me. I can sit behind the table on my camping chair and be ready to engage in conversation with people who come up to have a browse through the literature and often ask serious questions. There have frequently been several older team members on most Christian Answer missions, some in their seventies or beyond who, like me, find that they can serve in this way despite having limited physical energy.

For some of us, even this form of Christian service may become too much, as our bodies grow frail with age or disease, and strength and mobility decreases. But, if we are walking closely with the Lord and seeking to do His will each day, we will probably be spending more time in personal Bible study and prayer as we grow older, and in many other forms of service that perhaps a younger Christian may not have even considered. *Running* can be done on your knees interceding in prayer for others, sitting quietly meditating on God's word, or bent over a desk writing letters of encouragement to brothers and sisters in the Lord.

Amy Carmichael served as a missionary in India for fifty-five years from 1895 onwards, founding an orphanage that cared for hundreds of girls whom she had rescued from moral and spiritual danger as 'temple children'. These children had been dedicated to the gods by their parents, and would have ended up as temple prostitutes had she not intervened. After thirty-five years devoted to this work, at the age of sixty-three, Amy suffered an accidental fall down an unseen hole in the ground and sustained a severe injury to her spine. This resulted in her being almost totally confined to her room and in great pain for the last twenty years of her life. Did she feel that she was no longer able to run her race and that God had no further use for her in His service? While she may have felt frustrated at first by her physical limitations, she gradually grew to accept her condition, and, like the apostle Paul, was able to say that she had learned in 'whatever situation I am in, to be content' (Philippians 4:11). In those latter years of her life, she continued to supervise the running of the orphanage, spent much time in prayer, and wrote many books and poems, which have since been a source of inspiration and encouragement to thousands of readers. She was especially used by God to bring comfort in her writings to others who were also suffering physical illness or pain, able to understand what they were experiencing. She felt very strongly that God never 'lays a person aside', as if they were a broken cup that is good for nothing; rather, if God takes away someone's ability to perform a particular form of service, it is because He has other duties that He has for them to fulfil.[3] In the same way, if and when any of us become physically incapable of one means of service, we should not feel that we are *past our sell by date* and can no longer be of any spiritual use. Our mindset should always be: 'We make it our aim to please Him' (2 Cor. 5:9), and 'Whatever you do, do all to the glory of God' (1 Cor 10:31). However old or physically frail we are, our aim should still be to 'finish my

course with joy' (Acts 20:24, KJV). If this is our mindset, we shall indeed be running *at a good pace* right to the finishing line—the end of our race.

And what about when that end is actually in sight? None of us know when the exact time of our departure will be, but sometimes—

if for example we have cancer or an advanced chronic illness—we may become aware that we are in our last days, weeks or months on this earth. Our remaining time here is short. When Professor Verna Wright, a medical consultant and co-founder of United Beach Missions, was in the latter stages of prostate cancer, a well-meaning friend asked him if he thought that perhaps he should slow down in his Christian service and take things easy? Verna Wright's reply was short and to the point: 'When you see the finishing tape, you run faster!'

My own father also died of cancer in his mid-seventies. By the time the disease had been diagnosed, the cancer had spread and become inoperable. Informed of this, my father sought to share his faith at every opportunity. Whether it was a doctor or nurse visiting him at home on his sick bed, a neighbour, or the milkman who knocked at his door, my father sought to engage them in conversation about eternal matters. Were they, like him, ready to meet God, and did they know the Lord Jesus as their own Saviour and Friend? He knew that if the Lord had forgiven and saved *him*, then *anyone* could be saved!

Let us be like Verna Wright and my father, running with perseverance and finishing our course with joy.

> So we do not lose heart. Though our outer self is wasting away, our inner self is being renewed day by day. For this light momentary affliction is preparing for us an eternal weight of glory beyond all comparison, as we look not to the things that are seen but to the things that are unseen.
>
> For the things that are seen are transient, but the things that are unseen are eternal (2 Corinthians 4:16–18).

Chapter 9

Awake, my soul, stretch every nerve,
And press with vigour on;
A heavenly race demands thy zeal,
And an immortal crown.

A cloud of witnesses around
Hold thee in full survey:
Forget the steps already trod,
And onward urge thy way.

'Tis God's all-animating voice
That calls thee from on high;
'Tis His own hand presents the prize
To thine aspiring eye.

Blest Saviour, introduced by Thee,
Have I my race begun;
And, crowned with victory, at Thy feet
I'll lay my honours down.
(Philip Doddridge, 1702–1751)

10 Plans and purposes

The story of Joni Eareckson Tada, who sustained a severe spinal cord injury resulting in quadriplegia at the age of seventeen while diving into the sea at Chesapeake Bay in 1967, is well-known in Christian circles. Prior to her accident, Joni had been a very active teenager who enjoyed horse-riding and swimming. No doubt she had plans for her life which included remaining physically active, getting married and having children. But, in those few moments, her life changed forever. She spent two years in hospital undergoing rehabilitation following her injury and has remained a wheelchair user since that time. We have probably heard of others who were budding athletes, whose career in sport was brought to an end through injury. Some who have lost limbs may have eventually recovered sufficiently to return to running with the aid of prosthetic limbs, perhaps even participating in the Paralympics but, even if they did so, it was not what they had planned for when they first set out as a fit and healthy runner. Others, like Joni, are never able to walk again, let alone run.

As Christians, we may have faced circumstances in our lives when we felt that God was leading us into a particular sphere of service such as pastoral or missionary work, only to find that the door later seemed to close and prevent us from continuing along that path. God appears to have said 'No' to our plans to serve Him in the way that we had desired.

During my penultimate year in medical school, I had the opportunity of six-weeks work experience in a missionary hospital in Zaire (now known as the Democratic Republic of Congo). When I first felt, at the age of sixteen, that God wanted me to become a doctor, I thought that He may have plans for me to go and serve as a medical missionary in Africa. However, after I had gained my degree and qualified as a doctor, this sense of God's calling to such service in a foreign country felt less certain, and so I pursued my vocation on home soil. I worked for three years in various hospital posts in the UK and then one year as a trainee GP, acquiring the necessary skills and experience to become a General Practitioner. I also married Michael during this time (we had met at university where Michael was doing postgraduate studies in Physics), we bought a house and settled in a town in the north of England. I obtained a part-time GP post in the area, and subsequently we were blessed to have two children: a daughter, followed by a son two and-a-half years later.

I always felt that God had led me into the medical profession, and this sense of vocation helped me to persevere when at times the work was stressful and demanding. GP duties included some evenings and weekends 'on-call', and during those shifts I could never relax at home as I knew that at any moment my 'bleep' would sound and I would have to rush out in response to an urgent call. After our children were born, I found myself emotionally torn between my medical duties and my family responsibilities as a Christian mother, and often felt a little guilty about not always being at home when my children needed me. It was not easy finding suitable childcare for them when I was at work, and ensuring that I finished my duties in time to collect them from school, make the tea, help with homework and just be there for them became more stressful as they grew older. By the time our daughter was fourteen or fifteen years old, my symptoms of fatigue and exhaustion began to develop, and this eventually, after about eighteen months, led to me feeling unable to continue in my post as a GP. In 2002, I reluctantly handed in my notice at work, a little over twenty years after qualifying as a doctor. Initially, I hoped that, given time and some form of treatment, I would gradually recover and perhaps be able to later return to some form of medical work. I still worked one or two sessions a month at the local 'out-of-hours' centre to maintain my skills, but also for financial reasons, with the loss of my regular income being a significant concern in being able to provide for the family. As the months passed, my symptoms showed no real sign of diminishing, despite being able to rest more. I already had some knowledge of CFS from my medical training, but now I spent much time researching the condition and any possible therapy that claimed to either cure or significantly improve it.

After being referred to an NHS specialist in Liverpool in 2005, I was given their standard course of treatment, which involved Cognitive Behavioural therapy (CBT) and a graded exercise programme over a period of twelve to eighteen months. Sadly, while helping me to achieve a better understanding of CFS, it did little to alleviate my fatigue or other symptoms, and so I had to eventually accept the fact that it seemed unlikely I was going to recover. Rather, it would be a matter of learning to live with CFS by adapting my lifestyle and pacing myself. In 2007 I was successful in obtaining early retirement and a pension from the Health Service, and so at this point I stopped doing any further medical work. Over the following years I tried several forms of treatment for my illness, including physical, psychological and biological remedies, mostly provided by private practitioners and consequently incurring significant expenditure. One or two of these may have helped a small amount, but none of them produced a significant or lasting improvement. The problem with CFS is that, if you begin to feel a bit better and then start trying to do more, the increased activity can lead to a relapse in symptoms which could last for several weeks or even months. However, I could not see the point in sitting around doing very little, just in case I made myself worse—this kind of life seemed to be a waste. As one who was seeking to serve the Lord, I was desperate to feel better and to have more energy in order to serve Him. Why had this happened to me? Why had God seemingly prevented me from continuing in the work that He had originally called me into? I felt that, somehow, I had failed in my running of the race that God had marked out for me.

It has been a prolonged spiritual battle since then—one which is still not yet completely won—but by God's grace I do now feel that He has enabled me to be more accepting of my medical condition, and of the fact that God's plans and purposes for me are for my good and His glory. I am attempting to strike a balance between resignation and doing nothing on the one hand, and being discontent and continually searching for a cure for my CFS on the other hand. I seek to do what I can to maintain a degree of regular activity, while ensuring that I also take sufficient periods of rest and 'recreation' in order to recharge my batteries. This concept of managing symptoms and staying active—known as pacing—entails finding a baseline level of activity that can be maintained without any worsening of symptoms. The amount of activity can be very slowly increased over time and so, progress is made without triggering a 'boom or bust' cycle. By starting two or three years ago with a short walk each day, I am now able to run 4–5km, three times a week, and not suffer significantly for it. This has helped me to feel well enough in recent years to be involved with evangelistic work, both in my home church and on 'Christian Answer' missions, and also to teach in Sunday school. I have had to learn to say 'no' to certain things that I have felt would be too much for me, which has been a hard lesson to learn, but I am thankful to have progressed this far, with God's help.

King David had a great desire to build God a house, a temple fitting for God's dwelling place. He told the prophet Nathan of his plans, and he encouraged David to do whatever was on his heart, because

God was with him. However, God soon made clear to Nathan that it was not in *His* purposes for David to build the temple, but it was his son, Solomon, who would be given this task. David must have been disappointed when his plans, which seemed so good, were thwarted. But, although God said 'no', He also said to David: 'You did well that it was in your heart' (2 Chronicles 6:8). How kind God was to encourage His servant in this way, recognizing that David's desires stemmed from a heart that was truly seeking to serve Him. And David did not just give up at this point; he did all that was in his power to collect all the materials for building the temple and wrote down the detailed instructions for it to be made by Solomon. Near the end of his life, he was able to say to Solomon, 'I have prepared with all my might for the house of my God' (1 Chronicles 29:2–3, kjv).

Even if God has prevented any of us from pursuing a particular dream and appears to have said 'no' to our plans, we need to trust that

He always does so for a good reason. For Joni Eareckson Tada, we can see how God has used her greatly since her paralysis over fifty years ago. In her beautiful artwork painted by mouth, through her many encouraging Christian books, her ministry to people with disabilities through 'Joni and Friends', and simply by her inspirational example of perseverance and joy, God has been glorified. However, we may never know in this life what the reason was, but we must believe that God 'meant it for good' (Genesis 50:20). And we can still, like David, help to enable someone else to fulfil that task which we had longed to do, whether it be on the mission field or in some other sphere of Christian service. We can pray for God to send out labourers into His harvest field; we can give financially towards missionary work and encourage others in their service for the Lord. This does not mean that we have stopped running the race; rather, it simply means that God has changed the course of our race from what we had originally anticipated. We are still to run with endurance, but the race we are to run will be the one that *God has marked out for us*. Let us trust Him at all times and be content, remembering His word which says:

> For I know the plans I have for you, declares the Lord, plans for welfare and not for evil, to give you a future and a hope (Jeremiah 29:11).

> The heart of a man plans his way, but the Lord establishes his steps (Proverbs 16:9).

> Sovereign Ruler of the skies,
> Ever gracious, ever wise;
> All my times are in Your hand,
> All events at Your command.

His decree, who formed the earth
Fixed my first and second birth;
Parents, native place and time,
All appointed were by Him.

He that formed me in the womb,
He shall guide me to the tomb:
All my times shall ever be
Ordered by his wise decree.

Times of sickness; times of health;
Times of poverty and wealth;
Times of trial and of grief;
Times of triumph and relief;

Times the tempter's power to prove;
Times to taste the Saviour's love;
All must come, and last, and end,
As shall please my heavenly Friend.

Plagues and deaths around me fly;
Till He bids, I cannot die;
Not a single shaft can hit,
Till the God of love sees fit.
(John Ryland, 1753–1825)

11 Perseverance

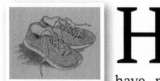

Have you ever been on a run when you seriously doubted if you were going to finish? Most of us who partake in running have probably experienced days when we had planned to go for a 5K run, but after a few minutes of slow but steady jogging we feel out of breath, our legs are aching and we feel like we will never succeed in reaching our planned destination.

In a physical race, we are dependent upon a number of factors in ensuring that we complete the course: being in a good state of health and fitness; having undertaken the necessary training; the weather conditions; not falling over or being tripped up by other runners. However well-prepared we are, we can never fully guarantee that some unforeseen circumstance will not occur during the race which prevents us reaching our goal.

In the Los Angeles Olympics of 1984, there was such an event on the final Friday evening of the competition. It was the women's 3000 metre final, in which the American athlete, Mary Decker, was the strong favourite to win the gold medal. Among the other competitors in the race was an eighteen-year-old South African girl named Zola Budd, who was running for Great Britain (South Africa was then banned from competition due to apartheid—Zola's grandfather was British, enabling her to gain British citizenship). Zola was relatively inexperienced as an international athlete and became famous for running her races barefoot. About halfway through the seven-and-a-half laps of the track, Mary Decker was in the lead. Zola Budd, close behind her, then took her chance to pass Decker and move to the front. As she cut into the lead, just in front of Decker, their feet caught each other, and Decker lost her balance and fell headlong. Her race was over. The photographs of Mary Decker sprawled on the track, looking in anguish at the other athletes disappearing into the distance, became infamous in sporting history. She could not have foreseen this unfortunate happening when preparing for the race.

But here lies the wonderful contrast when considering the Christian race—we *can* be sure of finishing! The reason for this certainty is because our confidence is not based on us, but entirely upon God. It is true that, as we have seen in previous chapters, there are various things that we have a responsibility to do in order for us to be able to run well, to be the best that we can be for the Lord. But however poor and faltering our race may at times be, the final outcome is never in doubt. If we are truly Christ's, we *will* complete the course, we *will* receive the reward.

How can we be so sure? By faith in the certainty of God's Word:

- Christ died for our sins (1 Corinthians 15:3).
- He rose again, for our justification (I Corinthians 15:4, 20; Romans 4:25).
- He ascended into heaven (Hebrews 9:24).
- He is preparing a place for us in heaven (John 14:2).
- He is at the right hand of the Father, interceding for us (Hebrews 7:25).
- He will come back to take us to be with him forever (Hebrews 9:28; 1 Thessalonians 4:16–17).

Jesus said, 'My sheep hear my voice, and I know them, and they follow me. I give them eternal life, and they will never perish, and no one will snatch them out of my hand. My Father, who has given them to me, is greater than all, and no one is able to snatch them out of the Father's hand' (John 10:27–29).

If you have come to Christ for forgiveness and trusted Him as your Lord and Saviour, then you are one of His sheep. He died for you; the price has been paid in full for all your sin. He is even now praying for you, interceding before the throne of God on your behalf. He is able to keep you from falling (Jude v. 24); you are in His hand and He will not let you go. You have an inheritance that is 'imperishable, undefiled, and unfading, kept in heaven for you' (1 Peter 1:4). And God is keeping you by His power, for that inheritance. What amazing security we have as believers in the Lord Jesus Christ!

Having this assurance of reaching heaven should not in any way make us complacent, thinking that it does not matter how we live if our reward is guaranteed unconditionally. Rather, it should spur us on to run faster—to 'press on toward the goal' (Philippians 3:14). It should make us desire to be more holy and Christlike in our lives, day by day. The apostle John, in his first letter, tells us that one day, when Christ appears, 'we shall be like him, because we shall see him as he is'. He then adds: 'everyone who thus hopes in him, purifies himself as he is pure' (1 John 3:2–3). Is this not why Jesus came to this earth and died for us? He 'gave himself for us to redeem us from all lawlessness and to purify for himself a people for his own possession *who are zealous for good works*' (Titus 2:14).

Peter also, in speaking of the future return of the Lord Jesus to judge the world and to take His people to be with Him for eternity, says, 'Since all these things are thus to be dissolved, what sort of people ought you to be in lives of holiness and godliness, waiting for and hastening the coming of the day of God' (2 Peter 3:11–12). Our eyes should be focused upwards, looking forward to that great day, and preparing for it even now by making it our aim always to please Christ (2 Corinthians 5:9). If we do this, then when our earthly race is finally over, 'there will be richly provided for ... [us] an entrance into the eternal kingdom of our Lord and Saviour Jesus Christ' (2 Peter 1:11).

> Come, let us anew
> Our journey pursue,
> Roll round with the year,
> And never stand still till the Master appear.
>
> His adorable will
> Let us gladly fulfil,
> And our talents improve,
> By the patience of hope and the labour of love.
>
> Our life is a dream;
> Our time, as a stream,
> Glides swiftly away,
> And the fugitive moment refuses to stay.
>
> O that each in the day
> Of His coming may say:
> I have fought my way through,
> I have finished the work Thou didst give me to do!

O that each from his Lord
May receive the glad word:
Well and faithfully done;
Enter into My joy, and sit down on My throne!
(Charles Wesley, 1707–1788)

Postscript

 **Y**es, *I did finally complete that Parkrun!* Eventually, the date for the return of the weekly *Parkrun* in the UK was announced and, on 24 July 2021, my dream was fulfilled when, along with my son and two granddaughters, I walked up the long slope to the start of my first run at Watergrove. I had heard how hilly and challenging this particular 5K course was, so I had mentally prepared myself for it and decided to walk up some of the steeper hills rather than overdo things. My aim for the first week was to try and complete the course in 40 minutes or less. The weather that morning was ideal for running—cool but dry, with just a slight breeze. I ran alongside my 10-year-old granddaughter, with my son and her older sister a few metres ahead, and we settled in towards the back of the field of eighty to ninety runners. I found that I definitely needed to walk up much of the uphill sections (they were tough!), but I enjoyed the downhill parts as well as the amazing views from the tops of the moors. As the course levelled off for the final stretch along the bank of the reservoir, I dug deep and managed to keep going and felt a real sense of achievement on crossing the finish line in a little under 39 minutes. Since then, I have remained sufficiently fit to complete a further 11 Parkruns and improved my personal best (PB) to 35 minutes, 32 seconds. I am so thankful to God for giving me the physical strength to keep going, and also for that initial message from my son, which inspired me to start running in the first place.

Postscript

Sept 22. I have now completed nearly 50 parkruns, and my PB at Watergrove is just under 34 minutes (although catching Covid 19 in early July set me back a little!).

But what of my spiritual race? I have not written this book as one who has already reached that conformity to Christ, which is God's ultimate purpose for His children, but as someone who is seeking to follow Paul's example:

> Forgetting what lies behind and straining forward to what lies
> ahead, I press on toward the goal for the prize of the upward call of
> God in Christ Jesus (Philippians 3:13–14).

When, by God's grace, I finally reach *that* goal, where I will see Christ and be made like Him, I will indeed *run and never be weary.*

It is possible that there may be a few of you who have been inspired by my running story, to either begin running, or to keep going as a runner. If that is the case, I will be glad. I am certainly a proponent of such physical activity for anyone to whom God has given sufficient physical health and strength.

But, much more importantly, even for those who are unable to run physically, it is my desire that by reading my words many of you will be encouraged in your spiritual journey, either to begin the race by putting your trust in Jesus Christ, or to keep persevering in the race until that day when faith will become sight. If my book accomplishes this or helps in even some small way, it will have served its purpose.

My dream: running with my two
granddaughters, Grace and Lois

With my son Nathan and granddaughter
Lois at a Parkrun

Endnotes

MY RUNNING STORY

1 Direct quote from the film *Chariots of Fire*, 20th Century Fox 1981

CHAPTER 5: PREDECESSORS

1 Zatopek, Emil, https://www.runnerstribe.com/an-athlete-cannot-run-with-money-in-his-pockets-he-must-run-with-hope-in-his-heart-and-dreams-in-his-head/

2 Pavey, Joanne, *This Mum Runs*, (New York: Vintage Publishing, 2017)

3 *The Song Book of the Salvation Army*, #586

CHAPTER 7: POWER

1 '8 Commandments of Good Running Nutrition', *Runner's World Magazine*, 14th July 2014, https://www.runnersworld.com/uk/nutrition/a772005/8-commandments-of-good-running-nutrition/

2 Spurgeon, C.H., *The Treasury of David*. Ed: Roy H. Clarke, (Nashville, Tennessee: Thomas Nelson Publishers, 1998), p. 1282

CHAPTER 8: PROBLEMS

1 Redpath, Alan, *The Making of a Man of God*, (Glasgow: Pickering and Inglis, 1962), p. 197

2 Redpath, Alan, *The Making of a Man of God*, p. 197

3 Ibid, p. 202

CHAPTER 9: PACE

1 Studd, C.T., https://gracequotes.org/quote/if-jesus-christ-be-god-and-died-for-me-then-no-sacrifice-can-be-too-great-for-me-to-make-for-him/

2 Elliot, Elizabeth [Editor], *The Journals of Jim Elliot*, (Ada, Michigan: Revell, 1978), p.173

3 Carmichael, Amy, *Rose From Brier*, (Fort Washington, PA: CLC Publications, 1980), p.36